TRADITIONS AND CELEBRATIONS

JUNETEENTH

by Lisa A. Crayton

PEBBLE
a capstone imprint

Pebble Explore is published by Pebble, an imprint of Capstone.
1710 Roe Crest Drive
North Mankato, Minnesota 56003
www.capstonepub.com

Library of Congress Cataloging-in-Publication Data is available on the Library of Congress website.
ISBN: 978-1-66390-348-8 (library binding)
ISBN: 978-1-66390-350-1 (paperback)
ISBN: 978-1-66390-351-8 (ebook PDF)

Summary: Juneteenth celebrates the emancipation of enslaved people in the United States. Across the country, people observe the day with speeches, parades, festivals, picnics, and family reunions. It is a day for people to come together and continue working toward equality. Readers will discover how a shared holiday can have multiple traditions and be celebrated in all sorts of ways.

Image Credits
Getty Images: Boston Globe/Contributor, 5, David Paul Morris/Stringer, 25, Go Nakamura/Stringer, 9, Jerry Holt/Star Tribune via Getty Images/Contributor, 19; iStockphoto: Bastian Slabbers, 1, 16, 17, kali9, 15; Library of Congress/The Alfred Whital Stern Collection of Lincolniana, 6; Newscom: Bob Daemmrich/ZUMA Press, 13, Peggy Paettie/ZUMA Press, 18; North Wind Picture Archives, 7; Shutterstock: Aaron of L.A. Photography, 20, AlexLMX, cover (flag), fitzcrittle, 23, Julian Leshay, 26-27, michaeljung, 12, Monkey Business Images, 4, 24, 14, New Africa, 8, Ozphotoguy, cover (background), Rawpixel.com, 11, Tippman98x, 10, 21, Trong Nguyen, cover (background), wavebreakmedia, 28, 29

Artistic elements: Shutterstock/Rafal Kulik

Editorial Credits
Designer: Sarah Bennett; Media Researcher: Kelly Garvin; Production Specialist: Spencer Rosio

TABLE OF CONTENTS

Words in **bold** are in the glossary.

ALL FREE

The United States has people of different **races**. We do not all look alike. We do not all sound alike.

Our differences are important. They make our country great. People can learn about each other. They can celebrate others' special days.

A community Juneteenth celebration in Boston

Juneteenth is a day to celebrate Black Americans. There are many ways to take part in the fun. Everyone is welcome!

A DAY TO CHEER

Have you ever been the last to hear good news?

In 1863, the **Emancipation Proclamation** was passed. This law freed **enslaved** Black people. But no one told the Black people in Galveston, Texas. They were the last ones to learn that slavery had ended.

Emancipation Proclamation

Military officers told people that slavery had ended.

More than two years later, Civil War soldiers came. They called everyone together. They gave one message: All people in the country were now free.

What a shock! The newly freed people shouted and danced. They had good reason to cheer.

Slavery was over. It had lasted almost 250 years. Thousands of Black people were badly hurt during slavery. As many as 1 million died. But no more.

Speakers share stories and lead cheers at Juneteenth celebrations.

People gather in Galveston at the site where enslaved people first learned of their freedom.

Freedom had come. The soldiers shared the news on June 19, 1865. A year later, people came back to Galveston. They celebrated freedom again.

It is still a day to cheer! It is called Juneteenth.

FAMILY TIME

Juneteenth is a holiday that celebrates freedom. Black Americans honor their history and **culture** with different activities. They invite other people to join them.

A Juneteenth celebration in Philadelphia

Many people spend Juneteenth as they do other holidays. They spend time with family. Some attend church or other faith services. They enjoy being with people who share their beliefs. They give thanks for the end of slavery. They talk about ways to keep making life better for everyone.

What are some other ways for families to celebrate? They might read books about Juneteenth. They can learn about famous Black Americans. They might watch videos or movies about Black history.

Family members gather for reunions on Juneteenth.

Some families gather for **reunions**. People may travel far to attend. They share meals. They play games together. They tell stories from long ago. Some families take time to visit the graves of relatives who have died.

Food is a big part of Juneteenth. Family and friends go to barbecues and picnics. They share dishes from **recipes** passed down by grandparents or great-grandparents.

Some people serve red food, juice, or soda. Red is a color that **symbolizes** freedom. It also stands for the blood and strength of those who were enslaved. The red drinks and food remind families what they are celebrating!

COMMUNITY FUN

Juneteenth is a holiday in most states. Many cities hold special events. Everyone is welcome. These events are free to attend.

People from the community are celebrated in Juneteenth parades.

Parades are a community favorite. They bring big crowds. People from the area also get to be in the parades! It is fun to see people you know riding on a big float. Other friends might show their talent marching, dancing, or playing an instrument. You could be in a parade too!

    Acting out past events can bring them to life. It is hard to imagine how things were long ago. Watching actors makes it easier to understand. Actors pretend to be soldiers. They might act out a Civil War battle. Then they give the good news that slavery has ended!

Museums set up special shows. They invite Black speakers to share their stories with others. Libraries invite authors to read books about Black lives.

Actors wear clothes from the past to act out events.

Music keeps people on their feet at Juneteenth celebrations. Musicians play old and new songs. Music is an important part of Black culture. **Spirituals**, jazz, and hip hop are all celebrated.

Musicians often perform at Juneteenth events.

Communities host festivals for Juneteenth. There are games, music, and lots of good food. What if your community does not have a Juneteenth event? There are celebrations online! Watch with your family. You will see performers and speakers from all around the country.

LEARN TOGETHER

There is a flag just for Juneteenth. It has the same colors as the U.S. flag: red, white, and blue. In the center is a big star.

The flag was created in 1997 by Ben Haith. He started the National Juneteenth Celebration Foundation.

In 2000, the flag was changed to how it looks today. It flies over state and city buildings on Juneteenth.

The Juneteenth flag

Some communities have youth programs for Juneteenth. Children might give speeches about the holiday. They might play a **trivia** game about Black history. They might listen to stories about the end of slavery.

Children take part in Juneteenth celebrations.

Have a Juneteenth party to celebrate freedom! Blow up red balloons. Let them float freely around the room. Draw Juneteenth flags on white paper. Tape them to the walls. Write poems on heart-shaped blue paper. Read them out loud!

People in the United States are learning more about Juneteenth. Many people celebrated the holiday in 2020 for the first time. Race problems made people think again about the **right** to freedom.

In 2020, many people marched on Juneteenth to honor Black lives.

Some companies wanted to honor the day. They felt it was important to show that Black lives matter. The National Football League made Juneteenth a holiday for its teams. Many stores made the day a company holiday.

Everybody can share in this special day. How will you celebrate Juneteenth? You can play games with your friends and family. You can have a picnic with your relatives. You can join a parade!

Slavery is over. Honor Black history. Celebrate Juneteenth!

GLOSSARY

culture (KUL-chur)—a group's beliefs or customs

Emancipation Proclamation (ih-man-sih-PAY-shun PROK-luh-MAY-shun)—a law that freed enslaved people in some states

enslaved (en-SLAYVD)—a person who is not free, who has been forced to be a slave

parade (pah-RAYD)—a public march to celebrate a special day, person, or event

race (RAYSS)—a major group into which people can be divided; people of the same race share common physical traits from their ancestry

recipe (REH-sih-pee)—instructions to follow for making food

reunion (ree-YOON-yun)—a family gathering

right (RITE)—a freedom that a person has that cannot be taken away

spiritual (SPEER-itch-oo-ul)—a religious, meaningful song first sung by enslaved Black people in the southern United States

symbolize (SIMM-buh-lyze)—to represent a certain thing or idea

trivia (TRIH-vee-uh)—short facts, often used in games to test knowledge

READ MORE

Cooper, Floyd. *Juneteenth for Mazie*. North Mankato, MN: Capstone, 2015.

deRubertis, Barbara. *Let's Celebrate Emancipation Day & Juneteenth*. New York: Kane Press, 2018.

Grack, Rachel. *Juneteenth*. Minneapolis: Bellwether Media, 2019.

Reader, Jack. *The Story Behind Juneteenth*. New York: PowerKids Press, 2020.

INTERNET SITES

Celebrating Juneteenth
nmaahc.si.edu/blog-post/celebrating-juneteenth

Holidays: Juneteenth
ducksters.com/holidays/juneteenth.php

Juneteenth: All About the Holidays
mpt.pbslearningmedia.org/resource/1cc3b3d6-6c27-442d-ba9d-c7a5fbf01ceb/juneteenth-all-about-the-holidays/

INDEX